SUSAN L. LINGO

Who's Who OBJECT TALKS that teach about the NEW Testament

23 Cool Characters Your Kids will Love

Standard®
PUBLISHING

Cincinnati, Ohio

DEDICATION

Listen, my dear brothers: Has not God chosen those who are poor in the eyes of the world to be rich in faith and to inherit the kingdom he promised those who love him?
James 2:5

Who's Who Object Talks That Teach About The New Testament
Copyright © 2003 by Susan L. Lingo

Published by Standard Publishing, Cincinnati, Ohio
www.standardpub.com

Credits
Produced by Susan L. Lingo, Bright Ideas Books™
Illustrated by Paula Becker
Cover design by Diana Walters
Typeset/Design Assistant: Lindsay Lingo

16 15 14 13 12 11   5 6 7 8 9 10 11 12 13
ISBN-13: 978-0-7847-1312-9
ISBN-10: 0-7847-1312-X
Printed in the United States of America

CONTENTS

INTRODUCTION

When it comes to the Bible and its myriad of stories and characters, kids' two favorite questions are:

Who's who, and what did they do?

Do you know who traveled over ten thousand miles or which simple girl God chose for the world's most important task? Or do you know whose name meant "son of encouragement" and who lived up to his name by encouraging Paul on his missionary journeys? You'll discover these exciting answers plus loads more in *Who's Who Object Talks That Teach About the New Testament!*

Who's Who Object Talks That Teach About the New Testament combines life-changing Bible truths with loads of cool characters who make the New Testament awesomely alive and relevant for kids today! Each message offers a memorable craft project, game, slick trick, or other concrete way to remember the who and the what behind each biblical person. And the nifty Who's Who collectible cards help kids recall in a snap who was who!

So have a ball presenting these memorable messages, fascinating facts, and awesome Bible enrichment fun to your kids as they memorably answer, "Who was who, and what did they do?" (Be sure to look for *Who's Who Object Talks That Teach About the Old Testament* for even more fun and fascinating Bible characters!)

➤ **Who's Who Cards:** These small, collectible cards are found on pages 46-48. Simply make as many copies as there are kids in class and cut out the cards as needed. Let kids punch holes in the tops of the cards and attach them to notebook rings, key chains, or large paper clips for instant flip-through review. Consider using the cards in games and other activities.

➤ **Who's Who Name Board:** Decorate the edges of a sheet of poster board using colorful characters from an old Bible storybook or coloring book. Laminate the poster, then use dry-erase markers or erasable crayons to write each Bible character's name as he or she is being introduced at message time.

WHO WAS THE WOMAN AT THE WELL?

John 4:7-14

Simple Supplies: You'll need a Bible, small paper cups, a bucket of water, two ladles, and copies of the Who's Who Woman at the Well card from page 48.

Before class, fill a bucket with cold water and place two ladles beside it at one end of the room. Be sure you have a small paper cup for each child. Small, bathroom-size cups will work fine. Place the cups beside the ladles. Finally, write the words "Woman at the Well" on the Who's Who board (directions on page 4) or on the chalkboard.

THE WHO & THE WHY

Form two teams and line up teams on the opposite end of the room from the bucket, ladles, and cups. Explain that in this relay the first players in line will each run and use the ladle to put water into a cup, then return the cups of water to the second players in line, who will drink the water. (The first "servers" will go to the end of the line and await their water.) After the second players drink their water, they will run to ladle water to serve the next players in line and so on. When everyone has had a drink of water, have the team shout, "We've been served!" and sit in place.

When everyone is seated, say: **That was great fun, and by now I'm sure no one is still thirsty. Water has always meant life for people. If we don't have water to drink, we will die. Jesus used water to teach a very important lesson to a woman in the New Testament. This woman was a Samaritan from the region of Samaria. One day the woman went to draw water from a well when Jesus was passing through. Jesus approached the woman and asked her for a drink of water. The woman was very shocked, because Jesus was a Jew, and Jews were never to associate with Samaritans. They were strictly forbidden to ever drink or eat from the same cup or bowl as a Samaritan. And here was a Jew asking for a cup of water! When the woman questioned why Jesus would ask her, Jesus had a surprising reply. Jesus told her that if she knew the gift of God and who was asking her for a drink, she would be the one asking him instead, and he would give her living water.** Read aloud John 4:10, then ask: **What do you think Jesus meant by this?**

Allow kids time to share their thoughts, then continue: **Jesus was telling the woman in a roundabout way that he was God's Son and that if she knew this, she would ask for his grace! Just think: Jesus was giving a clue as to** why he had come to earth and as to who he was! But the woman did not understand, so Jesus explained that the water that came from the well would help quench thirst for a while, but people would soon be thirsty again. Jesus told the woman that the living water from him would be eternal and that she would never thirst again. Read aloud John 4:13, 14. Ask: **What do you think Jesus was telling the woman?**

After kids share their ideas, say: **Jesus was explaining to the woman that if she would thirst for him and accept his love, she would be offered eternal grace, love, and life!** Ask:

➤ *In what ways is Jesus like living water to us?*

➤ *Why are we never thirsty again in our hearts and spirits when we accept Jesus into our lives?*

➤ *How do we think you can receive the living water of Jesus?*

Say: **When we are hurting or have troubles or wonder why we are on earth, we are thirsting in our hearts and spirits. We want help, and the only place that help to quench this thirst comes from is Jesus. When we drink in Jesus' love—or rather, accept his love and forgiveness into our lives—we don't thirst or hunger for truth or life again because we have all we need in Jesus. And all that Jesus offers us lasts forever and never runs dry. We may be thirsty again for plain old water, but we're never spiritually thirsty again when we accept Jesus into our lives!** Play the relay race again if you have enough water, then end with a prayer thanking Jesus for his living water that offers us eternal life.

Distribute the Who's Who Woman at the Well cards and invite a volunteer to read the card aloud. Punch holes in the corners of the cards and add them to the kids' Who's Who flip rings. If there's time, review any cards previously collected.

Who Was ZACCHAEUS??
Luke 19:1-10; 2 Corinthians 5:17

Simple Supplies: You'll need a Bible, black craft felt, tacky craft glue, scissors, a dollar bill, four quarters, gold satin cord, and copies of the Who's Who Zacchaeus card from page 48.

Before class, prepare a secret-pocket money sack by cutting a 10-by-4-inch rectangle and two 3 1/2-inch squares of black craft felt. Fold the ends of the long rectangle together and glue the two sides using tacky craft glue. This should form a pouch. Now glue the smaller squares inside the bag and against the sides to form secret pockets. (Only glue three sides of the squares to form the pockets.) Place four quarters in one of the secret pockets. During the object talk, you'll slyly slip the dollar in the other pocket, so keep track of which pocket the change is in and be careful not to jingle the change or let it escape! Cut an 8-inch length of gold cord and tie the money bag closed. Finally, write the name "Zacchaeus" on the Who's Who board (directions on page 4) or on the chalkboard. (If you plan to have kids make their own money bags, have extra craft felt and gold cord on hand.)

THE WHO & THE WHY

Hold the money bag you made earlier. (Be sure the quarters are hidden and don't jingle the bag or allow the quarters to slide out.) Ask kids if they know what you are holding. Allow kids to make their guesses, then say: **Long ago in New Testament times, people kept their money in money bags similar to this. Of course, most people back then didn't have a lot of money, and they were very careful to spend their money wisely. In Jesus' time, there were tax collectors who collected taxes from ordinary people to give to the king.** Hold up the dollar bill. **Tax collectors were not very popular, as you can imagine! And one tax collector in particular was disliked even more than the others. His name was Zacchaeus, and he made a habit of collecting more taxes than he needed to.** Carefully untie the cord and find the pocket where you plan to slide the dollar. Continue: **Zacchaeus would steal the extra money for himself and place it in his own money bag.** Slyly slide the dollar into the empty pocket and be ready to dump out the change without allowing the dollar to escape.

One day Zacchaeus heard that Jesus was coming to town, and he wanted to see this man whom everyone seemed to like and follow. But Zacchaeus was short and had trouble seeing from the ground, so he climbed the low branches of a sycamore tree to hide and watch. Imagine Zacchaeus's surprise when Jesus stopped under him and looked up. Jesus told Zacchaeus to come down, for they were going to have dinner at Zacchaeus's house! At dinner, Jesus forgave Zacchaeus for all the bad things he had done. Zacchaeus, who was used to being hated and despised, felt wonderful! Jesus had forgiven him, and Zacchaeus became changed! He was a new man! Zacchaeus, who had stolen money just a short time ago, now gave back four times what he had stolen! Shake the money bag to allow the four quarters to drop out. Hold the pocket with the dollar closed as you show kids the "empty" bag. Then ask kids to tell how the dollar bill changed. Say: **The dollar bill changed into, well, change! The dollar became like new, in a new form.** Ask:

➤ *In what ways did Zacchaeus change after meeting Jesus?*
➤ *How did Jesus change Zacchaeus?*
➤ *What changes were apparent in Zacchaeus's life after he was changed by Jesus?*
➤ *What changes happen in our lives when we accept Jesus and choose to follow him?*

Read aloud 2 Corinthians 5:17, then say: **Just as the dollar in our trick changed into change, Zacchaeus's life was changed into something new and wonderful by Jesus. And when we accept Jesus into our lives, we become changed and like new as well!**

If there's time, show kids how the trick was done and let them make their own money bags. Tell kids to borrow a dollar and four quarters at home and to present this object talk for their families and friends as a reminder of how our lives become changed when we accept Jesus.

Distribute the Who's Who Zacchaeus cards and invite a volunteer to read the card aloud. Punch holes in the corners of the cards and add them to the kids' Who's Who flip rings. If there's time, review any cards previously collected.

Did You Know?

Many early Christian writers claim the Apostle Peter appointed Zacchaeus as the head of the church in the ancient city of Caesarea.

Who Was JOSEPH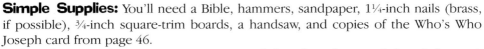

Isaiah 64:8; Matthew 1:24

Simple Supplies: You'll need a Bible, hammers, sandpaper, 1¼-inch nails (brass, if possible), ¾-inch square-trim boards, a handsaw, and copies of the Who's Who Joseph card from page 46.
Before class, cut the trim strip into an 8-inch length and a 5-inch length for each person plus a set for yourself. Make a wooden cross according to the directions in this object talk to show kids as a sample. Finally, write the name "Joseph" on the Who's Who board (directions on page 4) or on the chalkboard.

THE WHO & THE WHY

Hand each child an 8-inch and a 5-inch piece of trim board. Ask kids to gently rub their hands over the wood and describe how it feels. Then say: **Wood is rough when it hasn't been sanded, but rough wood can be used in so many ways to build things we can use. A carpenter takes rough wood and sees in it a finished building that will serve others. A piece of rough wood may become a chair to rest on, a bed to sleep in, or a house to protect people. A New Testament man named Joseph was a simple carpenter and, like a piece of rough wood, was used by God in amazing ways. The Bible doesn't tell us a lot about Joseph, but we do know he was a carpenter from Nazareth and** a distant descendant of King David. Joseph was chosen by God to be the stepfather of baby Jesus. Why? Perhaps because God saw in Joseph someone who would build a protective shield around Mary and Jesus and would tenderly raise Jesus with great love. God saw in Joseph a righteous man who loved and obeyed him. Read aloud Matthew 1:24, then continue.

Joseph was told by an angel in a dream that his wife Mary would give birth to the Son of God, and Joseph served God by protecting Mary and finding a place for God's Son to be born. Joseph obeyed the commands in another dream to protect baby Jesus by taking him to Egypt to escape death by King Herod. And when Jesus was older, Joseph brought his family back to Nazareth and taught Jesus about being a carpenter and lovingly working with wood. The last we hear of Joseph in the Bible is after he found Jesus in the temple teaching the elders.

Read aloud Isaiah 64:8. Say: **Just as clay is to a potter and wood is to a carpenter, we become molded in God's hands to be used by him.** Hold up the pieces of wood and say: **And Joseph was like wood to be built and formed into something precious in God's hands, too. Through his own carpentry, Joseph taught Jesus about preparing something rough and making it into something precious that could serve others—which is what Jesus did his entire life. Jesus molds, smoothes, and changes us so that we can be used by God to accomplish his will! Let's use this wood to make something precious to remind us of the role Joseph played in God's plans and in Jesus' life.**

Show kids how to nail the shorter pieces of wood across the longer sections to make wooden crosses. Then let kids use sandpaper to make their crosses smooth. As kids work, discuss how it must have felt to be Joseph, knowing your child was God's Son, and how great the responsibility was to teach Jesus and protect him with God's help. Have kids brainstorm ways that a carpenter is similar to what God builds in us. For example, a carpenter builds things from "nothing" as God helps us build our faith from scratch, and a carpenter works on pieces in individual ways as he completes his plans, which is how God works within each of us individually to complete his divine plans. When the crosses are complete, point out how the nail represents Joseph, who was at the crossroads between God and the earthly existence of Jesus.

Did You Know?

Oxen yokes were popular items for carpenters to make long ago. Jesus knew all about yokes when he spoke of them in Matthew 11:30.

Distribute the Who's Who Joseph cards and invite a volunteer to read the card aloud. Punch holes in the corners of the cards and add them to the kids' Who's Who flip rings. If there's time, review any cards previously collected.

Who Are ANGELS ? ? ? ? ?

Psalm 91:11, 12; Luke 1:19

Simple Supplies: You'll need a Bible, an angel figurine or ornament, foam board, paintbrushes, permanent markers, glitter glue, glow-in-the-dark paints, and copies of the Who's Who Angels card from page 46.

Before class, cut white foam board into 24-by-18-inch rectangles, one per child. Collect a variety of glow-in-the-dark paints (available at most craft stores). Finally, write the word "Angels" on the Who's Who board (directions on page 4) or on the chalkboard.

THE WHO & THE WHY

Hold up the angel figurine or ornament. Ask kids if they have angels around their Christmas trees and where they hang their angels. Then say: **It's during Christmas time when we see angels all around us. But the Bible tells us that angels are around us all of the time. Angels appear throughout the Bible and are given wisdom to know all things that are on the earth.** Read aloud 2 Samuel 14:20, then continue: **Angels are given two primary roles: to worship God and to carry out God's divine will on earth as his messengers. In fact, the word angels in Hebrew means "messengers." Angels are allowed to be in the presence of God, which means they are higher than people but not as high as the Lord.**

Read aloud Luke 1:19, then say: **We read many examples of how angels helped people in the Bible and how they carried out God's will. Angels announced the birth of Jesus and sang God's glory. They announced the birth of John the Baptist and told Mary and her friends that Jesus had been raised from death. Angels helped Daniel explain dreams to King Belshazzar and aided Peter in making an amazing escape from prison! And it will be the angel Gabriel who signals the end of time by blowing on his trumpet! Taa-daa!**

Angels are perfect examples of God's everlasting love for us! In fact, the word angel ends in the letters G-E-L (point to the last three letters in the word angel on the Who's Who board), **which you can remember stands for God's Everlasting Love! Angels watch over us and carry out God's plans on earth—even while we sleep!**

Invite volunteers to read aloud Psalm 91:11, 12, then let kids

Did You Know?

Treetop angels on a Christmas tree symbolize how angels proclaimed Jesus' birth from on high. For a fun reminder, sing "Angels We Have Heard on High."

make ceiling posters with glow-in-the-dark angels using the special paints and glitter. Use permanent markers to write the word angels on the poster, then add "God's Everlasting Love" below the appropriate letters. Tell kids to tape the posters to the ceilings over their beds as reminders of how God's guardians are watching over them.

Distribute the Who's Who Angels cards and invite a volunteer to read the card aloud. Punch holes in the corners of the cards and add them to the kids' Who's Who flip rings. If there's time, review any cards previously collected.

Who Were The GENTILES?
John 11:51, 52; Romans 3:29

Simple Supplies: You'll need a Bible, napkins, a platter or tray, tape, markers, and one paper flower and cupcake for each person. You'll also need copies of the Who's Who Gentiles card from page 46.

Before class, place the cupcakes on a tray or platter and set them at one end of the room. Finally, write the word "Gentiles" on the Who's Who board (directions on page 4) or on the chalkboard.

THE WHO & THE WHY

Make sure the platter of treats is at one end of the room. Set aside half of the paper flowers and the markers. Distribute the other flowers to half of the kids in class. Let kids tape the flowers to their shirts. Gather the kids at the end of the room opposite the treats and form two groups: one with flowers and one without.

Point to the word *Gentiles,* then say: **In ancient times, the word *Gentiles* meant "nations." The word referred to anyone not a part of one's own country or nation. For example, we are Americans, and everyone else in the world are "foreigners" to us. But if we lived in Africa and were Africans, Americans would also be called "foreigners." The word *Gentiles* was used much as we use the word *foreigners* today. Let's form our own pretend nations. Some of you are wearing paper flowers, so we'll call you the nation of "Flower-Powers." The rest of you will be called "foreigners" or "Gentiles."**

Now in Old Testament times, the Hebrews were a nation who worshiped God and to whom God had made many wonderful promises. Anyone who was not a Hebrew was a Gentile. When the tribe of Judah was formed within the Hebrews, they became known as the nation of "Jews," who were God's chosen people. All the other nations were Gentile because

they were not Jews. **God made wonderful promises that were meant only for the Jews. Let's make a neat promise to one of our pretend nations. The Flower-Powers will soon receive the promise of special treats at the end of room—see?** Point to the cupcakes. Continue: **Now this promise is for everyone who is wearing a paper flower. How do you feel about this?** Allow kids to share their thoughts, then say: **God made special promises to the Jews, but some of the Jews did not worship or obey God as he desired, and they did not accept Jesus as God's divine Son. So God chose to offer his promises of love, help, and salvation to all who choose to accept Jesus into their hearts and lives!** Read aloud John 11:51, 52 and Romans 3:29. Then ask:

> ➤ *How did God's acceptance of all people change the world?*
> ➤ *Why is it wonderful that God's promises and Jesus' salvation are for us all?*

Say: **No longer were God's special promises and Jesus' gift of forgiveness and eternal life only meant for one nation—they are meant for everyone who accepts Jesus as their Savior. And no longer are our special treats meant just for the Flower-Powers. Our special treats are for anyone who would like them!** Let kids choose their treats, then say a prayer of thanks for God accepting us all into his heart. Distribute the remaining paper flowers and have kids write "God's love is for us all!" on their flowers.

Distribute the Who's Who Gentiles cards and invite a volunteer to read the card aloud. Punch holes in the corners of the cards and add them to the kids' Who's Who flip rings. If there's time, review any cards previously collected.

Did You Know?

The same Greek word that the Bible translates "Gentiles" can also refer to anyone outside of the Christian church.

Who Were The WISE MEN?

Matthew 2:1, 2, 9-11

Simple Supplies: You'll need a Bible, tacky craft glue, glass votive holders, dried cloves and cinnamon-stick pieces, gold braid, scissors, incense cones, matches, and copies of the Who's Who Wise Men card from page 48.

Before class, prepare a special votive holder by gluing dried cloves and bits of cinnamon sticks to the sides of the glass. Glue gold braid around the top edge of the holder. Place an incense cone in the glass holder. (Bring a match to class to light the incense cone during message time.) Be sure to have extra craft materials and incense cones for kids to make their own special votive glasses. Finally, write the words "Wise Men" on the Who's Who board (directions on page 4) or on the chalkboard.

THE WHO & THE WHY

Light the incense cone and place the votive holder on the floor. Seat kids in a circle around the holder. As the scent begins to rise, ask kids to name the most special gift they have ever given anyone and to explain what made it so special. Then say: **We give special gifts to special people to show them how much they're loved and what they mean to us. Long ago, there were three gifts that were reserved for very special people: these gifts were precious gold** (point to the gold braid on the glass holder)**, a spice called "myrrh"** (point to the dried cloves and cinnamon sticks)**, and the scent of frankincense, which is what we're smelling right now.**

People gave these special gifts to show honor and respect to others. In the New Testament, these three gifts are men- tioned **in Matthew 2:11 as being presented to baby Jesus by wise men traveling from the east. No one knows for sure who these three strangers were, but most believe they were seers or kings from the east who had seen the beautiful, bright star God placed above Jesus' birthplace. We call these three wise men kings or "magi," who were from a group of people around the country of Persia who studied the stars and sought truth about God and the universe. The magi were not from Bethlehem but knew that something wonderful had happened and came in search of the one God had sent.**

The magi brought special gifts to honor the birth of Jesus. They brought gold, which symbolizes Jesus' kingship; they brought myrrh, which symbolizes Jesus being our heavenly Lord; and they brought frankincense, which rises upward as Jesus rose from death to live in heaven. The magi were the first Gentiles—or people who were not Jews—to honor and worship Jesus! Remember that the Jews were looking for so long for a beloved Messiah to be born, but it was the magi who recognized Jesus' miraculous birth and traveled so far to honor and worship him as God's Son. That is very special and reminds us that Jesus came for all who love, honor, and welcome him into their hearts and lives! Read aloud Matthew 2:11, then ask:

➤ *In what ways besides bringing gifts did the magi honor and worship Jesus?*

➤ *In what ways were these truly "wise men"?*

➤ *How can we honor Jesus in our own lives each day?*

Say: **When we give gifts at Christmas, we remember how the magi brought their own special gifts to honor and worship Jesus and how they wisely honored Jesus by seeking him. They honored Jesus by keeping him as the goal of their journey, even though their journey was long and per-haps difficult at times. And they honored Jesus by knowing he was a special gift from God sent to live among us. Let's make magi incense burners to remind us how the wise men came to honor Jesus and how we can do the same by seeking and worshiping him every day.**

Let kids use the craft items to make their own incense burners. Hand out the incense cones and tell children to have adults light the cones and blow them out during mealtime as a reminder of praising and honoring Jesus.

Distribute the Who's Who Wise Men cards and invite a volunteer to read the card aloud. Punch holes in the corners of the cards and add them to the kids' Who's Who flip rings. If there's time, review any cards previously collected.

Who Were The PHARISEES???
Psalm 103:12; Matthew 5:17-20

Simple Supplies: You'll need a Bible, markers, tape, and slightly enlarged copies of the scorecard from page 44. You'll also need copies of the Who's Who Pharisees card from page 47.

Before class, make a copy of the scorecard on page 44 for each person plus one enlarged copy for yourself. Tape the enlarged copy on the wall or chalkboard for kids to see. Place a marker close by. Finally, write the word "Pharisees" on the Who's Who board (directions on page 4) or on the chalkboard.

THE WHO & THE WHY

Gather kids in two teams in front of the scorecard on the wall and distribute the scorecards and markers. Explain that you'll play a game of Simon Says as you keep score. Tell kids to make a slash on their scorecards if their team breaks a rule. Explain that the team with no marks scored against them wins. As you play, continually mark teams down for silly rule "infractions" such as blinking eyes, giggling or talking, not turning around fast enough, or even for being too good a player. If kids protest your slash marks against them on the scorecard, mark them down again. Be sure kids are also marking their own scorecards!

Continue playing and marking slashes until both teams have several marks against them. Then have kids sit down in place. Point to the scorecard and say: **I guess with so many marks on the scorecard, neither team is a winner!** Ask:

➤ *What made playing this game so tough?*

➤ *How did adding more of my own rules to the basic game rules keep you from ever winning?*

➤ *Was this fair? Explain.*

Say: **During our game, there were the regular rules for Simon Says, and then there were the "rules" I added. What a recipe for failure! In New Testament times, there was a group of religious leaders called the "Pharisees" who were very strict with the rules or laws God had given through the Ten Commandments. But this group of leaders also added their own rules called "oral laws," which were often hard to remember and obey. No one could quite measure up to all of the Pharisees' silly rules! The Pharisees kept track of sins and broken laws just as someone keeps score on a scorecard. For example, God's law said to keep the Sabbath holy by not working on that day. The Pharisees then decided that actions such as moving a chair were work and could not be done. Would this make sense to you? Of course not! But if someone moved a chair on the Sabbath, they were found guilty of breaking the law. Zing—a mark on their spiritual scorecard!** Ask:

➤ *Could anyone live in a way pleasing to God with so many extra rules? Explain.*

➤ *How do you think Jesus felt about the Pharisees and their "score-keeping"?*

Say: **Jesus didn't get along very well with the Pharisees. He knew that God's laws were made by God alone and were made to help people live in harmony and peace with God and others. Jesus recognized that the Pharisees were judging people and making it impossible to obey God. Jesus wanted people to know God's truth and not just the oral laws of the Pharisees! You can imagine how angry this made the Pharisees, and they began to plot against Jesus to hurt him. Read aloud Luke 11:53, 54. Continue: Jesus wanted us to follow him when he told us that he alone is the way, the truth, and the life. Jesus made it clear that the Pharisees were not the final law!** Read aloud Matthew 5:17, 19, 20. Ask:

➤ *Why did Jesus not get along with the Pharisees?*

➤ *Who had the truth: Jesus or the Pharisees? Explain.*

Read aloud Psalm 103:12, then say: **Jesus came not to keep score against us but to forgive us and take away our sins!** Tear up the scorecard on the wall and toss it away. Have kids use their markers to write the words to Hebrews 8:12 across their scorecards: "For I will forgive their wickedness and will remember their sins no more." Tell kids to tape their scorecards to their walls at home to remind them that Jesus came to forgive us and not keep score as the Pharisees did.

Distribute the Who's Who Pharisees cards and invite a volunteer to read the card aloud. Punch holes in the corners of the cards and add them to the kids' Who's Who flip rings. If there's time, review any cards previously collected.

Who Was THOMAS ???

John 20:27-29; Hebrews 11:1

Simple Supplies: You'll need a Bible, empty tissue tubes or poster board, white paper, tape, markers, and copies of the Who's Who Thomas card from page 48.
Before class, prepare an I-Spy Tube by covering an empty toilet-tissue tube (or poster-board cylinder of the same dimensions) with white paper, then decorating it with colorful markers. (If you would like your kids to make their own tubes, collect enough tubes or have kids make tubes using poster board and tape. Make the tubes about 5 inches long and about 2 inches in diameter.) Finally, write the name "Thomas" on the Who's Who board (directions on page 4) or on the chalkboard.

THE WHO & THE WHY

Gather kids in a group and have your I-Spy Tube beside you. Play a quick game of I Spy using items in the room (and without using your spy tube yet). For example, you might say, "I spy a round item that keeps time." Let kids make their guesses, and when someone guesses a clock, let that player spy the next item. After several rounds, say: **It's easy to spy things around us when they are easily seen. We can see chairs, tables, people, the door, and tons more. But what if I said I spy a hole in my hand—would you believe me?** Wait for kids' responses.

Say: **It's very hard to believe what we can't see, isn't it? But let's see if you can see the hole in my hand as proof that it's there.** Hold the I-Spy Tube beside your open palm. Position your hand and tube as in the diagram. The optical illusion this creates will allow a "hole" to form in your hand. Let kids take turns seeing if their hands have holes in them. Then say: **Long ago in New Testament times, there was a man named Thomas, and he was one of Jesus' twelve original disciples. Thomas was with Jesus through all his miracles and was even there when Jesus died on the cross. But when Jesus was risen and showed himself to the other disciples, Thomas wasn't present and simply wouldn't believe that the others saw Jesus! Thomas said he wouldn't believe it unless he could put his fingers through the nail marks on Jesus.** Ask:

➤ *Why was it hard for doubting Thomas to believe what his friends had seen?*

➤ *Why did Thomas want to touch the nail holes before he would believe?*

➤ *What does this tell us about Thomas's faith?*

Continue: **A week later, the disciples and Thomas were gathered together in a room. The door was locked, but Jesus came in and greeted them all. Then Jesus told Thomas to touch the nail holes in Jesus' hands and commanded Thomas to stop doubting and believe!** Ask:

➤ *What did Jesus' words "stop doubting and believe" mean?*

➤ *Why do you think Jesus let Thomas feel his wounds?*

➤ *Do you think Thomas believed then? Explain.*

Say: **Thomas did believe—finally! But Jesus went on to say some of the most powerful words he ever spoke.** Read aloud John 20:29, then ask:

➤ *What did Jesus mean when he said, "Blessed are those who have not seen and yet have believed"?*

➤ *What does Jesus teach us about faith and not having to see with the eyes to know with the heart?*

➤ *How can having this kind of faith help us draw closer to Jesus?*

Say: **Our I-Spy Tube let us "see" with our eyes, just as Thomas had to see the holes in Jesus' hands and side. But Jesus wants us to have the kind of faith that believes without seeing.** Read aloud Hebrews 11:1, then continue: **Just as we can't see the wind, we know it is real. Just as we don't see our hearts beat, we know as long as we live that they do! We know because we have faith and see what is accomplished by the wind or by beating hearts. We may not "see" faith, but we know what faith can do! Let's end with a prayer asking Jesus for the kind of faith that believes without having to see.** Share a prayer asking Jesus for greater faith, then end by reading aloud John 20:29 once more. If kids make I-Spy Tubes of their own, have them write the words to John 20:29b on the tubes.

Distribute the Who's Who Thomas cards and invite a volunteer to read the card aloud. Punch holes in the corners of the cards and add them to the kids' Who's Who flip rings. If there's time, review any cards previously collected.

Who Was **MARY?** ? ? ?
Luke 1:46-49

Simple Supplies: You'll need a Bible, Epsom salts, flower-shaped candy sprinkles, self-sealing sandwich bags, ribbon, plastic spoons, a measuring cup, scissors, markers, and copies the "Thank You, Mom!" card from page 45. You'll also need copies of the Who's Who Mary card from page 47.
Before class, gather enough Epsom salts and flower-shaped candy sprinkles for kids to make bath-salts bags to present to their moms. Each bag will need to hold ¾ cup

of Epsom salts and a plastic spoonful of candy sprinkles. Prepare a bag of bath salts according to the directions below to show kids. Finally, write the name "Mary" on the Who's Who board (directions on page 4) or on the chalkboard.

THE WHO & THE WHY

Gather kids and explain you have a riddle that describes a person. Hold up the bag of Epsom salts and tell kids that this bubble bath gives a hint to the riddle. Then say:

I'm not a sister or a brother,
But I'm part of every family.
I give you love and laughter and life—
In fact, you can't be born without me!
Who am I?

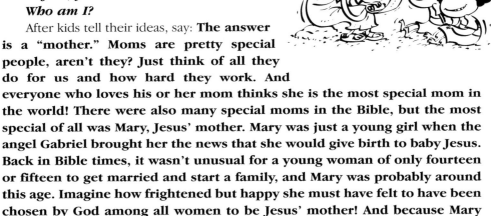

After kids tell their ideas, say: **The answer is a "mother." Moms are pretty special people, aren't they? Just think of all they do for us and how hard they work. And** everyone who loves his or her mom thinks she is the most special mom in the world! There were also many special moms in the Bible, but the most special of all was Mary, Jesus' mother. Mary was just a young girl when the angel Gabriel brought her the news that she would give birth to baby Jesus. Back in Bible times, it wasn't unusual for a young woman of only fourteen or fifteen to get married and start a family, and Mary was probably around this age. Imagine how frightened but happy she must have felt to have been chosen by God among all women to be Jesus' mother! And because Mary loved and trusted God, she became his willing and thankful servant. When Mary learned she would become Jesus' mother, she gave great thanks to God in a song called the "Magnificat."** Read a portion of the Magnificat or Mary's Song from Luke 1:46-49 (or more if time allows).

Continue: **Mary helped raise Jesus, protecting him, loving him, teaching him, and marveling at how Jesus grew in God's grace. But Mary also knew her time with Jesus would be short. And even though she knew the world would harm her son someday, she continued to trust and love God and hold Jesus in her heart—just as a loving mother would do! It was Mary who encouraged Jesus to perform his first miracle at Cana in changing water to wine. And Mary was the only relative of Jesus' to be present at his crucifixion on the cross. Think of how hard that must have been for Mary! Before Jesus died, he asked his disciple John to care for his mother. And it's thought that Mary lived with Jesus' beloved disciple until her death at the age of seventy-two.** Ask:

➤ *Why do you think God chose Mary to be Jesus' mother?*
➤ *What qualities made Mary a wonderful mother to Jesus?*

➤ *In what ways did Mary have the hardest "mothering" job of any mom in the world?*

➤ *How can you thank your own mom for being loving and kind to you?*

Say: **Mary was kind, loving, protective, encouraging, and faithful to her son, Jesus. I'm sure Jesus thanked Mary in many ways for her love and tenderness. We can thank our own moms, too, to remind us how Mary was God's willing servant and how our own moms serve our families with love and devotion.**

Have kids prepare special bags of bath salts by measuring ¾ cup of Epsom salts into each bag and mixing in one plastic spoonful of flower-shaped candy sprinkles. Explain that moms can pour half of their bath salts under the running bath water to soften the bath. (The candy sprinkles will melt in the hot water and leave no stickiness behind.) Then let kids color the gift-card poems and attach them to the bags along with pretty ribbons.

Distribute the Who's Who Mary cards and invite a volunteer to read the card aloud. Punch holes in the corners of the cards and add them to kids' Who's Who flip rings. If there's time, review any cards previously collected.

Who Were The SHEPHERDS

John 10:15, 27

Simple Supplies: You'll need a Bible, a scarf to use as a blindfold, a piece of fleece or sheepskin fabric, poster board, tape, markers, and copies of the Who's Who Shepherds card from page 48.

Before class, use a marker to divide the poster board into two columns. Label the top of one column "Shepherds" and the other column "Jesus." Tape the poster board to the wall where kids can see it. Make sure you have a small piece of sheepskin fabric of fleece such as a lamb might have. Finally, write the word "Shepherds" on the Who's Who board (directions on page 4) or on the chalkboard.

THE WHO & THE WHY

Hold up the piece of sheepskin or fleece and say: **This is a bit of fluffy fleece that is much like a shepherd would have seen on his sheep. Let's use this**

fleece to play a game about shepherds and lambs. Clear a playing area in the center of the floor and choose one child to be the "lamb" and one to be the "shepherd." Have the shepherd tell the lamb his name and recite "Mary Had a Little Lamb" so that the child playing the lamb can learn the "shepherd's" voice. Have the rest of the kids form a large circle around the lamb and blindfold the child playing the lamb. Place the piece of fleece somewhere in the circle on the floor and position the shepherd outside of the circle. Explain that in this hunt-n-find game, the shepherd can walk around the outside of the circle giving directions to the lamb that will lead the lamb to the fleece. The other kids will try and mislead the lamb by giving phony directions such as "turn left" when the lamb really needs to go straight ahead. Tell the lamb it will be easier if he crawls on the floor and listens very carefully to the voice of his shepherd. Continue the game until the lamb finds the fleece or until three minutes have passed. After the game, ask:

➤ *Why was it difficult for the lamb to find the fleece quickly?*

➤ *Why was listening for the shepherd's voice so important?*

➤ *In what ways is this game like following Jesus in the midst of our often-confusing and wicked world?*

Say: **This game showed us that it's not easy being a lamb or a kind shepherd! The Bible mentions shepherds many times and in many ways throughout both the Old and New Testaments because that is what many people did for a living back in Bible times. But Jesus also referred many times to shepherds in his teachings. Let's discover more about how shepherds cared for their sheep and how Jesus is the Good Shepherd who cares for us.** Gather kids in front of the poster board and have a marker ready. In a moment, you will use the table at the bottom of page 21 as a guide for what to list on the poster-board columns.

Say: **A shepherd's life was filled with hard work and worry for his flocks. He was constantly on guard and moving to find good grazing lands and water for his flocks because the shepherd knew that food and water were essential to life. The good shepherd led his sheep to good life.** On the shepherd's column on the poster board, write "led in the right way." Continue: **If a sheep or lamb was weak or sick, the shepherd would often carry it to keep up with the flock and to give it rest.** Write "gave rest" below the first item you listed.

Say: **A shepherd worked hard to protect every one of his sheep from dangers such as wolves, lions, and bears. In fact, the good shepherd would lay down his life for his sheep.** Write "laid down life for sheep" on the list under the shepherds column.

Continue: **Sheep knew who cared for them, and sheep in a flock knew the voice of their shepherd and followed him.** Write "sheep know voice and follow" on the list. Say: **And at night, a good shepherd played softly on his flute or harp to soothe the sheep and make them calm and peaceful.** Write "calmed and gave peace" on the list. Say: **Good shepherds were simple, kind, and caring people. They weren't concerned with how rich they were or how they dressed. They were not kings and royalty, yet God chose to tell these simple shepherds before anyone else about the birth of Jesus! Angels came to the shepherds in their fields to tell them the good news, and shepherds were the first to seek Jesus and worship him!** Ask:

➤ *Why do you think shepherds were the first to know about Jesus?*
➤ *Why were shepherds so important to every lamb in the flock?*
➤ *In what ways are we like the sheep in Jesus' flock?*

Form five groups and assign each group one of the following verses to read. Then decide which shepherd quality corresponds to the verse about Jesus and write a portion of the verse in the correct place on the "Jesus" column. (Refer to the chart at the bottom of the page.)

➤ *John 14:6*
➤ *Matthew 11:28*
➤ *John 10:15*
➤ *John 10:27*
➤ *John 14:27*

When the lists are complete, read aloud John 10:11, then say: **Jesus called himself the Good Shepherd, and now that we have learned about the importance of shepherds we realize more what this means. Jesus calls and seeks us, and because we love him we want to follow him. Jesus protects and helps us and gives us rest and peace in troubled times. And Jesus laid down his life to forgive us so we could have the gift of eternal life! Wow! Jesus is our Good Shepherd, and we are his sheep who want to love and follow him forever!**

Distribute the Who's Who Shepherds cards and invite a volunteer to read the card aloud. Punch holes in the corners of the cards and add them to the kids' Who's Who flip rings. If there's time, review any cards previously collected.

SHEPHERDS	JESUS
➤ led in the right way	➤ led as the way, truth, life (John 14:6)
➤ gave rest	➤ gives rest to weary (Matthew 11:28)
➤ laid down life for sheep	➤ laid down life for sheep (John 10:15)
➤ sheep know voice and follow	➤ sheep know voice and follow (John 10:27)
➤ calmed and gave peace	➤ calms and gives peace (John 14:27)

Who Was MARTHA ? ? ? ?

Luke 10:38-42; John 11:5

Simple Supplies: You'll need a Bible, prepared apple juice, brownies or cupcakes, and party supplies, including balloons, crepe paper, paper plates, and cups. You'll also need copies of the Who's Who Martha card from page 47.

Before class, prepare the room for a small party by hanging several balloons and crepe-paper streamers around your "party table." Set the table with paper plates and cups and place the juice and a plate of brownies or cupcakes in the center. Finally, write the name "Martha" on the Who's Who board (directions on page 4) or on the chalkboard.

THE WHO & THE WHY

Welcome kids warmly with hugs, then gather them around the party table. Explain that you want to celebrate the many people of the Bible who teach us so many wonderful truths and ways to love the Lord. Then quietly serve each child a brownie and cup of apple juice. When everyone is served, offer a prayer thanking God for all the ways his people have taught us through their own examples of faith and serving. Then enjoy the treats as you discuss the following questions.

➤ **What three things did I do to make this party happen?** (Lead kids to tell that you prepared the party, welcomed the party goers, and served the treats.)

➤ **How did I prepare for our party?**

➤ **How did I welcome you to join in**?

➤ **How did I serve you?**

After the treats are eaten, say: **I did three important things to put on our party. I prepared, I welcomed, and I served. In the New Testament, we read of a woman named Martha who did these same three things when she knew Jesus was going to visit her. Martha lived with her sister Mary and her brother Lazarus in the city of Bethany, which was close to Jerusalem. Martha, Mary, and Lazarus were good friends with Jesus, and whenever Jesus was teaching or healing nearby in Jerusalem, he would stop in to visit. Martha was probably the oldest of the three siblings, and she was very concerned that things be nice for Jesus. So she would clean and fix delicious meals for him, she would welcome Jesus warmly into her home, and she would serve Jesus when he was visiting by providing good meals and friendship alongside her sister Mary and brother Lazarus.**

Read aloud Luke 10:38, 39. Continue: **One time when Jesus visited, Martha became frustrated because she was doing all the work while her sister Mary** just sat and listened to Jesus. **But Jesus gently reminded Martha that Mary had chosen to do what is so important, too—she had chosen to listen and learn from Jesus. It was a reminder that listening and honoring Jesus quietly is also a way to serve him—one of the very best ways!** Read aloud Luke 10:40-42.

Ask kids why it's important to learn from Jesus, then continue: **Martha loved Jesus and trusted in him, so when her brother Lazarus became sick and died, Martha sought Jesus' help—and Jesus raised Lazarus from the dead in an amazing miracle! Why do you suppose Jesus performed this amazing miracle for Martha, Mary, and Lazarus?** Read aloud John 11:5, then continue: **Martha spent her entire life preparing for, welcoming, and serving Jesus, as did her sister and brother. What wonderful lives dedicated to Jesus!** Ask:

➤ *In what ways did Martha's preparing for, welcoming, and serving Jesus express her love for him?*
➤ *What did Martha teach us about the ways we can honor Jesus in our own lives?*

Say: **Martha taught us a great deal about serving Jesus, but she also learned an important lesson herself: Take time to learn about Jesus and to listen to God! We can prepare for Jesus to live in our hearts. We can welcome Jesus into our lives each day, and we can serve Jesus by helping others. Finally, we can also honor Jesus by quietly listening to him and learning. Let's quietly honor Jesus with a prayer right now.** Pause for a minute, then quietly offer a prayer expressing your love to Jesus and your desire to serve him throughout your lives.

Distribute the Who's Who Martha cards and invite a volunteer to read the card aloud. Punch holes in the corners of the cards and add them to the kids' Who's Who flip rings. If there's time, review any cards previously collected.

Did You Know?

The name "Martha" comes from an Aramaic word that means "lady of the house."

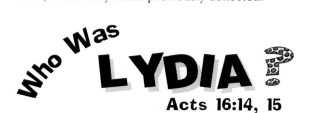

Who Was LYDIA?

Acts 16:14, 15

Simple Supplies: You'll need a Bible, a purple shower-curtain liner or purple fabric, scissors, glitter, gold braid, paint pens (from craft stores), a 15-inch dowel rod for each person (¼-inch diameter), and a stapler. You'll also need copies of the Who's Who Lydia card from page 47.

Before class, gather craft supplies for each person. You'll need a purple shower-curtain liner or purple cotton fabric cut into 14-by-22-inch rectangles, one per person. Cut 2-foot lengths of gold braid, one for each person. Kids will be making purple banners to hang on their front doors. Finally, write the name "Lydia" on the Who's Who board (directions on page 4) or on the chalkboard.

THE WHO & THE WHY

Hold up a piece of purple liner or fabric and say: **How many of you like the color purple? It's such a bright and vibrant color and is often associated with royalty. Long ago in Bible times, it was much the same. Purple was a precious color for fabric and was very costly. Only the wealthiest people could afford purple cloth. In the New Testament, there was a woman named Lydia who sold purple cloth in the city of Philippi. She was a sound business woman who became very wealthy from the beautiful cloth she sold. Lydia was a Gentile who loved God but didn't know Jesus. She didn't know, that is, until Paul came to Philippi, and Lydia listened to him teach and preach the Good News about Jesus and his gift of salvation. Lydia listened to Paul and was so moved by the power of his message about Jesus that she asked to be baptized immediately.**

Lydia became the first person outside of the area Jesus had lived in to become a Christian! Lydia was so happy to know the truth about Jesus that she carried the message of his forgiveness and salvation to her family, and they were soon baptized as well! Lydia offered her home to Paul for a place to stay when he was in Philippi, and later Lydia opened her home so the first Christian church and community could meet there safely. Lydia was a wonderful example of accepting Jesus into her life, then spreading the Good News of his love to those closest to her so they could know Jesus' love, too. Ask:

➤ *In what ways did Lydia express her love for Jesus?*
➤ *How was offering her home to Paul and the other Christians an act of great love and generosity?*
➤ *What does Lydia teach us about choosing to serve Jesus? about spreading the Good News of Jesus' salvation?*

Read aloud Joshua 24:15a, then say: **Choosing to love and follow Jesus is a powerful decision. Jesus doesn't force us to love or follow him—he desires us to want him in our lives. And just as Lydia made the choice to love and follow Jesus and help her family serve Jesus, so can our families!**

HOUSEHOLD
AS FOR ME AND MY
LORD
WE WILL SERVE THE

Let kids make banners to hang on their front doors to show how they desire to open their homes to others in Jesus' name. For each banner, fold the top edge of the rectangle (the 14-inch side) over a dowel rod and staple the material in a "hem" over the rod. Tie a 2-foot length of gold braid to the ends of the dowel rod as a hanging loop. Using paint pens, write the words "As for me and my" up the left side of the banner, as in the illustration. Write the word "household" across the top edge, and the words "we will serve the" down the right side of the banner. Finally, write the word "LORD" down the center of the banner. Sprinkle the wet paint with glitter, then set aside to dry.

Distribute the Who's Who Lydia cards and invite a volunteer to read the card aloud. Punch holes in the corners of the cards and add them to the kids' Who's Who flip rings. If there's time, review any cards previously collected.

Who Were The APOSTLES?
Matthew 4:19; 1 John 4:19

Simple Supplies: You'll need a Bible, white copy paper, markers or crayons, and copies of the Who's Who Apostles card from page 46.

Before class, draw the following message based on 1 John 4:19 on a sheet of white copy paper using markers or crayons. Plan to have your class present or teach their message to the kids in another room at the end of this message. Finally, write the words "Apostles/ Disciples" on the Who's Who board (directions on page 4) or on the chalkboard.

THE WHO & THE WHY

Distribute paper and markers or crayons to kids, then have them form groups of three. Tell groups to choose members to be player A, player B, and player C. Have all the A players stand at the front of the room, all the B players stand in the center of the room, and all the C players stand at the back of the room. Explain that in this relay game you will teach the A players a message using words and pictures. When they have learned the message, they will go to their B players and teach them the message in words and pictures. Finally, the B players will teach the C players the message. When the C players have learned and written the message, have them hold up their papers and shout, "Message learned!"

Begin the game by showing the A players how to draw the pictures to the words, "We [smiling faces] love [heart] because [arrow] he [cross] first [1st symbol] loved [heart] us [smiling faces]." Have A players draw the pictures and repeat the words until they are learned. Then have those players teach the message to their corresponding B players and so on. When all of the C players have their papers raised, let each one read the message on the paper aloud. If the message is correct, give high fives to each team. If the message isn't correct, have teams reteach the message.

Say: **That was fun! Our relay game involved two important actions: learning and teaching. We learned an important message, then told and taught that message to someone else until we all knew the message! Long ago, Jesus called twelve very special people to be special learners called "disciples." Jesus first called two fishermen brothers named Peter and Andrew to follow him.** Read aloud Matthew 4:19, then continue: **In other words, Jesus wanted to teach his disciples how to reach other people with God's truth. These were the first two disciples or learners. The other ten were:**

James, John, Bartholomew,
Philip, Thomas, and Matthew,
Another James, then Thaddeus,
Simon, and finally Judas.

The Twelve were called "disciples" because they were pupils learning about Jesus and about God's power and truth. And when Jesus knew they were ready, he sent them out as the twelve apostles to carry the truth as messengers. The Greek word for disciple means "learner or pupil," and the word apostle comes from a Greek word that means "ambassador or messenger." You see, the twelve first had to learn as pupils; then they could preach and teach the message to others as apostles! The twelve came from different walks of life. Peter and Andrew were fishermen, and Matthew was a tax collector. Jesus chose his special pupils to be the first to witness his powers and miracles and to be taught directly by him about faith, prayer, serving others, healing, and much more. And it is through the twelve apostles that we learn about Jesus and all he offers us. The apostles spread Jesus' message and gospel far and wide and helped set up the first church congregations. Jesus commanded the apostles to pray, heal, teach, preach, work miracles, and baptize in his name.

However, one of the original disciples—Judas—betrayed Jesus. He sold Jesus to be killed for thirty pieces of silver. Judas felt so guilty at betraying Jesus that he eventually hung himself. It's believed that the other original apostles, all except John, were eventually killed as martyrs of the faith. They died serving Jesus because they wouldn't deny the truth—that Jesus is the Son of God! Ask:

▶ *In what ways are we disciples, learning about Jesus?*

➤ *In what ways can we become Jesus' apostles, messengers for God?*

➤ *Why is it often more difficult being an apostle than being a disciple? Is it worth it? Explain.*

Say: **Now that we've learned an important message about Jesus' love for us, let's become apostles and carry this message to the kids in another room so they may become disciples and learn why we want to love Jesus and others!** Go to another class and pair your kids up with partners to teach them the rebus verse from 1 John 4:19.

Distribute the Who's Who Apostles cards and invite a volunteer to read the card aloud. Punch holes in the corners of the cards and add them to the kids' Who's Who flip rings. If there's time, review any cards previously collected.

Did You Know?

Paul is often called the thirteenth apostle because he saw Jesus in a vision and taught others about Jesus as he set up the first Christian churches.

Who Was PAUL?

Acts 9:3-5, 17-20

Simple Supplies: You'll need a Bible, a copy of the ovals on page 44 for each child, and copies of the Who's Who Paul card from page 47.
Before class, make one copy of the ovals on page 44 for each child. You may also wish to find a map of Paul's missionary journeys to hold up and show kids as you name some of the places Paul visited to establish churches. Finally, write the name "Paul" on the Who's Who board (directions on page 4) or on the chalkboard.

THE WHO & THE WHY

Gather kids in a circle and distribute the copies of the oval handout. Invite kids to tell about something that was so amazing they could hardly believe their eyes, such as a neat trick, an unexpected good grade on a paper, or a surprise gift they received. Then say: **Sometimes we may see or experience something that makes us hardly believe our eyes! Not only may our views and thoughts be changed, but our lives may be changed as well. In the New Testament, a man named Saul experienced a life-changing event that made him hardly believe his eyes. As I tell you more about this important biblical person, I want you to stare at the black oval on your paper. Don't stop staring at the oval until**

I tell you to. Then we'll see what you see on your paper and if you can believe your own eyes.

Saul grew up as a tentmaker in the city of Tarsus. He was a Jew who loved God very much. Saul was very intelligent and studied under Gamaliel, the most learned teacher of Jewish law. After Jesus died on the cross and was risen again, Saul had become a Pharisee—an upholder of Jewish law. Saul hated Jesus' followers because they seemed to go against Jewish law. In fact, Saul hated Jesus' followers so greatly that he persecuted them, arrested them, and even had them killed for loving Jesus! Keep staring at your ovals.

Then one day an amazing event changed Saul's life forever. As he was traveling to Damascus, a city outside Tarsus, Saul fell to his knees when he saw something that he could hardly believe! What did Saul see? Look quickly at the white portion of your paper. What do you see? Kids should see a very bright light or glowing oval. Say: **Saul saw a blinding, glowing light that filled his eyes. And then Saul heard a voice ask, "Saul, why do you persecute me?"** Read aloud Acts 9:4, then continue: **Jesus had spoken to Saul, and Saul was blinded because of his spiritual blindness. But when Saul knew he was speaking to Jesus, he repented and obeyed Jesus, and soon his sight was restored.**

Read aloud Acts 9:17-20, then continue: **Jesus changed Saul's name to Paul. But his name wasn't the only thing that had changed—Paul's life was forever changed through Jesus! Paul dedicated his entire life to serving Jesus by teaching others about Christ's love and salvation and by establishing the first Christian churches. Paul was called "the apostle to the Gentiles"—those who were not Jews. Paul's mission was to teach and preach the Good News to the Gentiles so all could know Jesus as their Savior. Paul made five missionary journeys around Asia Minor and even to Rome, which is in Europe. The letters we read to these churches make up a great portion of the New Testament.** Have kids find the following epistles in their Bibles: Romans, 1 and 2 Corinthians, Galatians, Ephesians, Philippians, Colossians, and 1 and 2 Thessalonians. **Paul spent his life serving, loving, and following Jesus and spent many months in jail as he tried to bring the Good News to Gentiles. Paul couldn't believe his eyes at one point in his life but couldn't believe how he was blessed for the rest of his life!** Ask:

➤ *In what ways did Paul's life change when he was blinded on the road to Damascus?*

➤ *How are our lives changed when we accept Jesus into our hearts and lives?*

Did You Know?

Paul traveled over ten thousand miles during his missionary journeys. Now that's what I would call going the extra mile for Jesus!

➤ *How did Paul demonstrate his love for Jesus?*
➤ *In what ways can we be like Paul right in our own families, schools, and town?*

Distribute the Who's Who Paul cards and invite a volunteer to read the card aloud. Punch holes in the corners of the cards and add them to the kids' Who's Who flip rings. If there's time, review any cards previously collected.

Who Was LAZARUS ????
John 11:26, 35

Simple Supplies: You'll need a Bible, a deck of playing cards, white paper, scissors, tape, and a red marker. You'll also need copies of the Who's Who Lazarus card from page 47.

Before class, cut a piece of white paper to fit a playing card and tape the paper to one of the cards. On the false card front, use a red marker to write the name "Lazarus" and to draw a heart below the name. Next, use scissors or a knife to cut a rectangle in the center back of the card box. Make the rectangle about ¹⁄₂ inch wide by 2 inches long. Slide the false card into the box with the card back facing the cut slit. Find the two red queens and the jack of hearts and place them in the order of queen, queen, jack on top of the other cards. Slide the cards into the card box on top of the Lazarus card. During this message, you'll need to keep the Lazarus card in the box, being very careful not to let kids see either the slit or the hidden card! At the appropriate time, you will place all the cards in the box so they're sitting in front of the hidden Lazarus card. Then you will simply slide your index finger up the slit to "raise" the Lazarus card. Finally, write the name "Lazarus" on the Who's Who board (directions on page 4) or on the chalkboard.

THE WHO & THE WHY

Be sure the two queens and jack are the first three cards on top of the deck in the card box. Gather kids in front of you and hold the deck of cards. (Remember: Don't let kids see the back of the deck or the hidden card!) Remove the cards, being careful to leave the hidden Lazarus card in the box. Set the card box cut-side down.

Say: **I have an amazing story to tell you about someone from the New Testament named Lazarus who was greatly loved by both God and Jesus. We'll use these cards to help. Lazarus lived in the village of Bethany, near Jerusalem, and was the brother of Martha** (remove a queen from the top of the deck and place it on the floor) **and Mary** (remove the other queen and lay it on the floor.) **This was a different Mary than Jesus' mother. Lazarus and his two sisters were very close friends of Jesus** (remove the jack of hearts and place it on the table). **Jesus would often visit Mary, Martha, and Lazarus when he was nearby in Jerusalem.**

Once, when Lazarus became very ill, his sisters sent for Jesus, who was helping others in the town of Perea. The sisters wanted Jesus to come heal Lazarus, but Jesus couldn't come at that very moment. When Jesus heard that Lazarus had died, he came to Bethany and was sad in spirit. In fact, Jesus felt so sad, he wept.** Invite a volunteer to read aloud John 11:35, then continue: **This is the shortest verse in the Bible, but a very powerful one. John 11:35 says, "Jesus wept." And in his sadness, Jesus gathered Mary and Martha and went to Lazarus's tomb.** Gather up the cards, shuffle them once, then place them in the card box in front of the hidden Lazarus card.

Say: **Mary and Martha told Jesus that Lazarus had been dead for four days. Jesus called to have the stone rolled away from the tomb. Then, in a loud voice, Jesus called to his friend to come out—and Lazarus was raised from the dead!** Slide the Lazarus card up from the back of the deck and remove it. Continue: **This miracle was so amazing that it convinced many who saw it that Jesus was indeed the Messiah. Some of the Jewish priests, though, worried that Jesus would make trouble for them, so from that moment on they plotted how they could get rid of Jesus. The miraculous raising of Lazarus was cause for great joy and points us to the deep truth that only Jesus can conquer death. And through our loving and accepting Jesus into our lives and hearts, we are offered the gift or eternal life, too!** Read aloud John 11:26. Ask:

➤ *Why do you think Jesus wept at the death of his beloved friend?*
➤ *How did Mary and Martha demonstrate their love for Lazarus? their faith in Jesus' power to help?*
➤ *In what ways does Jesus offer us love and eternal life as he did when he raised Lazarus from death?*

Say: **Lazarus's name is a form of the Hebrew name "Eleazer," which means "one whom God helps." And through Jesus, God brought Lazarus back from death. The Lord gave new life to Lazarus, and he offers us new life through his loving forgiveness and salvation.**

Distribute the Who's Who Lazarus cards and invite a volunteer to read the card aloud. Punch holes in the corners of the cards and add them to the kids' Who's Who flip rings. If there's time, review any cards previously collected.

Who Was PETER ???

Matthew 16:18; Acts 2:33

Simple Supplies: You'll need a Bible, paint pens, tacky craft glue, craft felt, scissors, and a large smooth stone for each person. You'll also need copies of the Who's Who Peter card from page 47.

Before class, cut two 1-inch squares of craft felt for each person. Kids will be gluing the felt squares to the bottoms of the stones to use as paperweights. Finally, write the name "Peter" on the Who's Who board (directions on page 4) or on the chalkboard.

THE WHO & THE WHY

Seat kids in a circle. Hold up a large, smooth stone and say: **This rock is strong and solid, tough to break or crumble, and this rock reminds me of a New Testament Bible character whose name means "rock" in Greek. As we discover more about Peter, the rock, we'll pass these rocks around the circle. When I say "Stop passing," hold on to your rock and hold it high if you can answer the question I ask. Then we'll continue passing the rocks.** Distribute the rocks and begin passing them around the circle.

Say: **Peter and his brother, Andrew, were fishermen in a small village long ago. Jesus invited both Peter and Andrew to follow him and become fishers for people. Jesus wanted Andrew and Peter to become his first disciples. Stop passing.** Ask:

➤ *Who was Peter's brother, and what did they do for a living?*
➤ *In what ways did the disciples become fishers of people?*

Continue passing the rocks and say: **Peter was a big burly guy and a bit shy. But he loved Jesus and wanted to be a good disciple. Peters real name was Simon, but Jesus renamed him Peter, which meant "rock" in Greek. Peter was destined to become a strong and solid force for Christians and churches in the future, but he had a lot of growing to do! Stop passing.** Ask:

➤ *In what ways do you think Peter might have needed to grow?*
➤ *How does growing in faith and trust help us become strong, solid Christians?*

Pass the rocks and continue: **Peter was the first person Jesus asked about his being God's Son, and Peter recognized him as our true Lord. Another time Peter tried to walk on the water out to Jesus but took his eyes from Jesus and began to sink. Jesus caught Peter and told him he had little faith. Peter was also the disciple to deny he knew Jesus three times before the sun rose on the day Jesus was crucified. After his death and resurrection, Jesus** forgave Peter and asked him to feed his sheep, meaning that Peter was to teach people the Good News of salvation. **Stop passing.** Ask:

➤ *How did Peter struggle with his faith and trust in Jesus?*

➤ *How does struggling with faith help it become even stronger?*

Pass the rocks and say: **Peter's faith continued to grow until Jesus told him, "You are Peter, and on this rock I will build my church"** (Matthew 16:18). **After Jesus was risen from death, he sent the Holy Spirit to his followers. Peter, filled with the Spirit, spoke boldly and bravely about Jesus. The Spirit had changed a shy guy to a bold witness for Christ!** Read aloud Acts 2:33, then continue: **And just as Jesus had predicted earlier, Peter became the rock on which the Christian church was being built. Peter became the apostle to the Jews and brought the truth of Jesus and his salvation to Jewish community. At the end of his life, though, Peter was crucified upside-down on a cross for his faith and missions work for Jesus. Stop passing.** Ask:

➤ *In what ways did Peter express his love and faith in Christ even after Jesus was risen to heaven?*

➤ *How can we live as Peter lived, with growing faith and helping others know Jesus?*

Say: **Peter began as a shy and sometimes bumbling disciple, but through his growing faith and love for Jesus he became a powerful force in forming Christ's church. And Peter didn't stop growing or going for Christ his entire life! Let's embellish rocks that remind us of Peter and the strong, rock-solid faith we can grow just as Peter did!**

Have kids use colorful paint pens to write the following based on Psalm 62:7, 8: "The Lord is my rock—trust in him always!" Glue felt squares on the bottoms of the rocks so kids can use the rocks as paperweights without scratching tables or desks.

Distribute the Who's Who Peter cards and invite a volunteer to read the card aloud. Punch holes in the corners of the cards and add them to the kids' Who's Who flip rings. If there's time, review any cards previously collected.

Who Was STEPHEN ?

Acts 6:8, 9, 15; 7:51-53

Simple Supplies: You'll need a Bible, a tape recorder, a blank tape, and copies of the Who's Who Stephen card from page 48.

Before class, be sure you have batteries or an electrical outlet for the tape recorder. Record the following Scripture selections from Acts to play during mes-

sage time (pause for a moment after each reading): 6:8; 6:9; 6:15; 7:51-53. Finally, write the name "Stephen" on the Who's Who board (directions on page 4) or on the chalkboard.

THE WHO & THE WHY

Set up the tape recorder and be ready to play the verses at the appropriate times. Ask kids to tell what a "witness" is and why a witness can be very important during a trial. Say: **A good witness can tell truthfully the events surrounding an incident. A witness tells what he saw and heard to help people who weren't present. As Christians, we are witnesses by telling others about the glorious truth of Jesus and his message of love and salvation. In the New Testament, there was a man named Stephen who was a powerful witness for Christ and who eventually died for teaching others about Jesus. Stephen was the first Christian martyr, that is, someone who died teaching others about Christ. Long ago a witness had only his voice for people to listen to, but today we have CDs, televisions, radios, and tape recorders to record our witness and tell our stories. Let's use this tape recorder to discover more about Stephen and why his witness was powerful enough to get him killed as a martyr for Christ.**

Play the first verse you recorded earlier (Acts 6:8), then say: **Stephen was a Jew who had seen and heard the things Jesus had done is his life. Stephen knew that Jesus was God's Son and that his people had killed Jesus on the cross. The Holy Spirit filled Stephen and helped him tell others the truth about Jesus and his salvation. But Jewish leaders became angry over Stephen telling about Jesus, and they planned to do away with Stephen to stop his teaching.** Play the next portion of the tape (Acts 6:9). Then ask:

➤ *Why do you think the Jewish leaders were so worried about the gospel message?*

➤ *Why was Stephen such a threat to the Jewish leaders?*

➤ *Would you have stopped telling others about Jesus? Explain.*

Continue: **When the Jewish leaders arrested Stephen and he stood before them, what do you think they saw?** Play the third portion of the recording (Acts 6:15). Say: **They saw that Stephen's face was like that of an angel. The Holy Spirit was truly with Stephen! And then Stephen delivered his most powerful witness or speech to the leaders. Stephen reminded them about obedience to God through Abraham, Moses, and Joshua. Then Stephen boldly accused the leaders of unfaithfulness and disobedience to God for killing Jesus on the cross.** Play the final portion of the recording (Acts 7:51-53). Ask:

➤ *Why did Stephen tell the leaders they were disobedient to God?*

➤ *How do you think the Jewish leaders felt when they heard Stephen's bold speech?*

Say: **The Jewish leaders were furious and took Stephen outside the city walls, then killed him by stoning him to death. Stephen died for his unwavering and powerful faith in Jesus.** Ask:

➤ *Was it worth dying for to tell others about Jesus? Explain.*

➤ *What can we learn from Stephen and from his brave and bold witness about Jesus?*

➤ *Who could you boldly and bravely witness to about Jesus today?*

Say: **Stephen became the first Christian martyr and taught us about the importance of telling others about Jesus no matter what! We can tell others about Jesus right now by recording one or two thoughts you have or things you would like to say about Jesus or the way Jesus has changed your life. Let's take turns recording, then we will play back our witness messages.**

Did You Know?

Saul (Paul) watched the stoning of Stephen. Perhaps God was planting the seeds of Saul's faith by his witnessing of Stephen's own unwavering faith!

After recording and listening to your messages, consider playing the tape for another class or making copies of the tape for kids to take home as a powerful reminder of witnessing boldly for Jesus as Stephen did.

Distribute the Who's Who Stephen cards and invite a volunteer to read the card aloud. Punch holes in the corners of the cards and add them to the kids' Who's Who flip rings. If there's time, review any cards previously collected.

Who Was JOSEPH OF ARIMATHEA

John 19:38-42

Simple Supplies: You'll need a Bible, 10-inch cheesecloth squares, a stapler, scissors, dried potpourri, cinnamon or clove oil, and copies of the Who's Who Joseph of Arimathea card from page 47.

Before class, make a potpourri sack by cutting a 10-inch square of cheesecloth, folding it in half, and stapling three sides together. Place a small handful of dried potpourri in the bag, then drop several drops of cinnamon or clove oil on the potpourri. Finish by stapling the open edge closed. (You'll need enough potpourri, oil, and cheesecloth squares for each child to make a sack.) Finally, write the name "Joseph of Arimathea" on the Who's Who board (directions on page 4) or on the chalkboard.

THE WHO & THE WHY

Seat kids in a circle and tell them to close their eyes. Pass the scented sack under their noses and ask them what they smell. Then have kids open their eyes and say: **Mmm! Some scents are so pleasing and fragrant, aren't they? This scented cloth sack reminds me of how tenderly Jesus was anointed and wrapped in soft cloth after his death on the cross. But who cared so much for Jesus? Who wanted to help him after his death and after so many people wanted to hurt him?**

A man named Joseph, who came from Arimathea, was the man who cared so much for Jesus. Joseph of Arimathea was a wealthy Jew who secretly followed Jesus when he was alive. Joseph recognized that Jesus was not like others, and after listening to Jesus teach and heal others, Joseph of Arimathea knew Jesus was God's Son. But Joseph was a member of the Sanhedrin, the Jewish religious leaders, and he couldn't tell anyone how much he loved and respected Jesus. It hurt Joseph greatly when his own people killed Jesus on the cross, and it took great bravery to ask for Jesus' body from Pontius Pilate, the Roman governor who agreed to Jesus' death.

Read aloud John 19:38, then continue: **Joseph of Arimathea and his friend Nicodemus, who also secretly followed Jesus, gently took Jesus' lifeless body away from the cross. They tenderly anointed his body with aloes and myrrh, very expensive spices and oil. Then they lovingly wrapped Jesus' body in soft cloth and placed him in a new tomb that Joseph of Arimathea had purchased for himself. Finally, they rolled a stone in front of the opening to the tomb and sadly left. Just think: It was Jewish leaders who allowed Jesus to be hung on the cross, yet it was also a Jewish leader who so tenderly cared for Jesus and provided a place for Jesus to be buried.** Ask:

➤ *Why do we know that Joseph of Arimathea truly cared for and respected Jesus?*

➤ *In what ways did Joseph demonstrate his love for Jesus?*

➤ *How can we show Jesus that we love and care for him, too?*

Say: **Joseph of Arimathea wasn't the sort of man you would think would provide so tenderly for Jesus. After all, he was a member of the group who didn't approve of Jesus or his teachings. But Joseph recognized the authority with which Jesus taught and healed, and Joseph spent many hours visiting with Jesus and getting to know him. Just as Joseph sought out Jesus** to learn from him, we can, too. We can show Jesus we love and care for him by seeking him in our own lives and by seeking his teachings so we can learn to live as he desires us to live. Let's make scented sacks to remind us of the tender love Joseph of Arimathea felt for Jesus and how we can love Jesus just as sweetly.

Have kids make their own scented sacks, then end with a prayer telling Jesus of your love and expressing your desire to learn from him as Joseph of Arimathea learned.

Distribute the Who's Who Joseph of Arimathea cards and invite a volunteer to read the card aloud. Punch holes in the corners of the cards and add them to the kids' Who's Who flip rings. If there's time, review any cards previously collected.

Who Was The CENTURION???
Matthew 8:5-13; 17:20

Simple Supplies: You'll need a Bible, an index card, tape, a sunflower seed, a pumpkin seed, a mustard or radish seed, and copies of the Who's Who Centurion card from page 46.

Before class, tape the seeds to an index card in order of size. (If you are using a radish seed, pretend it is a mustard seed, since it will be referred to as a mustard seed during the object talk. The two seeds are fairly close in size, although a mustard seed is still smaller than a radish seed.) Write the name "Roman Centurion" on the Who's Who board (directions on page 4) or on the chalkboard.

THE WHO & THE WHY

Gather kids and show them the seed card. Explain that there is a mustard seed, a sunflower seed, and a pumpkin seed taped to the card. Ask kids to tell you which seed might grow the biggest plant and why. Then say: **Three seeds in three different sizes. It would seem like the bigger the seed, the bigger the plant. But you might be surprised to know that the smallest seed in God's creation grows one of the biggest, strongest of plants! This is exactly how Jesus said our faith can grow—that even if our faith is as small as a mustard seed, it can move mountains!**

In the New Testament, we learn about the growing faith of a man who didn't know God or Jesus but who had only heard about them. This man was a Roman centurion, a soldier for the army of Rome. Now, Romans didn't believe in God and wouldn't accept Jesus as God's Son. So when the Roman centurion came to find Jesus one day, everyone was

greatly surprised! The Roman centurion told Jesus his servant was very ill and asked Jesus to heal his servant. The centurion was very humble and told Jesus he was used to being the one in command, but he knew that Jesus' authority was far greater. He had faith that Jesus could help and heal his servant. Jesus was astonished at the Roman centurion's faith! After all, he had not been raised to love God, yet here he was asking Jesus for help and being assured that Jesus had the power to heal his servant! Ask:

> ➤ *Why do you think the Roman centurion chose to ask Jesus for help and not a Roman doctor or someone else?*
> ➤ *In what way did the Roman centurion show how great his faith in Jesus was?*
> ➤ *How do you think Jesus responded to the centurion's request for help?*

Say: **Jesus told his disciples that the Roman centurion had greater faith than anyone in Israel! And Jesus immediately healed the centurion's servant. Because the Roman centurion had great faith and because he sought Jesus and asked for his help, his servant was healed through Jesus' power.** Ask:

> ➤ *What can we learn about having faith from the Roman centurion?*
> ➤ *Why is it important to seek Jesus and to ask for his help when we need it?*
> ➤ *How does turning to Jesus for his help demonstrate our faith in him?*

Say: **The Roman centurion taught us a great lesson about having faith, and Jesus teaches us that even if we have faith only as big as a tiny mustard seed, we can move mountains!**

Distribute the Who's Who Roman Centurion cards and invite a volunteer to read the card aloud. Punch holes in the corners of the cards and add them to the kids' Who's Who flip rings. If there's time, review any cards previously collected.

Who Was The POOR WIDOW??

Matthew 25:40; Mark 12:41-44

Simple Supplies: You'll need a Bible, a collection plate, two pennies, a dollar bill, and copies of the Who's Who Poor Widow card from page 48.
Before class, place the two pennies and the dollar bill in an offering plate. Finally, write the words "Poor Widow" on the Who's Who board (directions on page 4) or on the chalkboard.

THE WHO & THE WHY

Gather kids and hold the offering plate. Say: **This collection or offering plate has some money in it given by two people. One person gave two pennies, and another person gave a dollar. Who do you think gave more and why?** Encourage kids to discuss and share their views and thoughts, then say: **The answer seems obvious, doesn't it? It would seem as if the person who gave the greatest amount of money gave the most—but maybe there is another way to look at this question!**

Long ago in New Testament times, Jesus visited the temple in Jerusalem. Many people were milling around by the temple, and most were dressed richly because they had a lot of money. Jesus and his disciples watched the collection box as many rich people threw in large amounts. Then a poor widow came and put in two very small coins. The copper coins amounted to only a fraction of a penny. Ask:

> ➤ *Who gave more generously: the rich people who gave a great deal or the poor widow who gave two pennies? Explain.*

Say: **Jesus turned to his disciples when the poor widow had gone and told them that the widow gave much more than the rich people because she gave all she had to give. Jesus pointed out that the rich people gave out of their wealth, while the poor widow gave out of her poverty and gave all she could.** Ask:

> ➤ *What did Jesus mean when he said the widow gave out of her poverty?*
> ➤ *In what ways did the widow show her generous spirit and unselfish heart?*
> ➤ *Is there ever a good excuse for not sharing or giving to help others? Explain.*

Say: **Jesus taught us that giving is measured not by what is given but by how it is given. When we have much and give much, it is wonderful. But when we have little and give all we have, that is even better! The poor woman gave her coins to help others, and in so doing she gave to Jesus. Listen to what the Bible tells us about giving to others and Jesus.** Read aloud Matthew 25:40, then say: **When the widow gave from her heart to help others, she was also serving Jesus and expressing her love for him. We can give money like the widow, too, but there are more ways to give and share with others.** Ask:

> ➤ *What are ways we can give to others and, in so doing, give to Jesus?*

Did You Know?

The holiday song "Little Drummer Boy" has the same theme as this widow. Sing the song, then tell how it is similar to the story of the widow's offering.

➤ *Who can you give to this week through your time, money, help, prayer, or encouraging words?*

End message time by sharing a prayer asking Jesus to help you give from your love in different ways this week to help others and serve him.

Distribute the Who's Who Poor Widow cards and invite a volunteer to read the card aloud. Punch holes in the corners of the cards and add them to the kids' Who's Who flip rings. If there's time, review any cards previously collected.

Who Is The HOLY SPIRIT ?

John 14:26; 16:7-14; Acts 2:1-4

Simple Supplies: You'll need a Bible, white paper, markers, red and yellow food coloring, newspapers, plastic drinking straws, and copies of the Who's Who Holy Spirit card from page 46.

Before class, collect white paper and a plastic drinking straw for each person plus one for yourself. If you have very young kids, you may wish to provide paint shirts. Cover a table with newspapers. Finally, write the name "Holy Spirit" on the Who's Who board (directions on page 4) or on the chalkboard.

THE WHO & THE WHY

Gather kids around the table and place a sheet of white paper on the newspaper. Place a drop of red food coloring on the paper and blow it into a squiggly flame shape. Then add a yellow drop of food coloring where you placed the first drop and blow it into a flame shape over the red as closely as possible.

After you've made a flame, ask kids to tell you how the colors traveled around the paper without a paintbrush to drag them. (Kids will eventually tell you it was the air you blew from the straw that moved the food color.) Then say: **You said that air blew the colors around, but I didn't see any air. How do I know air was working on the colors? Because I could see what the result was! We could all see that the colors were traveling and moving over the paper. Sometimes we cannot see something, but we know it is real by what it accomplishes. This is how it is with the Holy Spirit. We cannot see him with our eyes, but we see what he accomplishes through us. As we discover more about who the Holy Spirit is and what he does for us, we'll work on special pictures as reminders of his power in our lives.** Distribute white paper to each person along with a straw and marker.

Say: **Remember when Jesus was baptized in the River Jordan? After his baptism, the Holy Spirit descended like a dove to sit above Jesus,** and God expressed his pleasure in Jesus' obedience. **The Holy Spirit was present at Jesus baptism, but we didn't need his help because Jesus was on earth among people at that time. Not long afterward, Jesus promised he would send us a special Counselor and friend—the Holy Spirit.**

Read aloud John 14:26, then have kids use markers to write "the Holy Spirit" across the tops of their papers. Continue: **After Jesus was risen to heaven, the disciples were gathered in Jerusalem when a sound like the rushing of wind blew into the room.** Have kids blow through their straws in the air. Say: **The disciples saw tongues of flame come down to rest above them, and they were filled with the Holy Spirit. Jesus' promise of the Spirit had been kept to us!** Have kids blow one flame using red and yellow food coloring as you continue: **Jesus sent us the Holy Spirit to help us on earth and to guide us. Listen as I read all that the Holy Spirit does for us as you blow another flame or two.**

The Holy Spirit was sent to testify about Jesus and to help us tell others about Jesus, too. Read aloud John 15:26, 27. **The Holy Spirit was sent to convict the world of sin and guilt, of righteousness and judgment.** Read aloud John 16:7-11. **The Holy Spirit was sent to guide us in all truth and to tell what is to come. Read aloud John 16:13. And the Holy Spirit was sent to bring glory to Jesus and to share all truth with us!** Read aloud John 16:14. Then have kids use markers to write "He will guide you in all truth" across the bottoms of their papers. Ask:

➤ *In what ways does the Holy Spirit help us do the things Jesus would do if he were on earth in person?*
➤ *How do we know the Holy Spirit is our friend and helper?*
➤ *In what ways is the Holy Spirit a gift of Jesus' love to us?*

Say: **The Holy Spirit is our friend and Counselor. He is our guide and helper. And the Holy Spirit is the one who strengthens our faith and shows us ways to help others and serve Jesus. What a friend we have in the Holy Spirit!**

Let kids finish blowing a few more red and yellow flames across the centers of their papers. Then set the papers aside to dry as you share a prayer thanking Jesus for sending us the gift of the Holy Spirit.

Distribute the Who's Who Holy Spirit cards and invite a volunteer to read the card aloud. Punch holes in the corners of the cards and add them to the kids' Who's Who flip rings. If there's time, review any cards previously collected.

Who Was JOHN THE BAPTIST?

Matthew 3:1-6; John 1:29, 34

Simple Supplies: You'll need a Bible, a bowl with softened cream cheese, honey, pitted whole dates, plastic knives, napkins, newsprint, markers, tape, and copies of the Who's Who John the Baptist card from page 46.

Before class, mix softened cream cheese and honey together in a bowl. Stuff a pitted date with the cream-cheese mixture for each person. Use a black marker to write the following list of "firsts" on a sheet of newsprint: first to call for repentance and washing away of sins; first to recognize Jesus as Lord; first to identify and call Jesus the Son of God; first to die in association with Jesus. Tape the newsprint to a wall where kids can see it and have a blue marker handy. Finally, write the name "John the Baptist" on the Who's Who board (directions on page 4) or on the chalkboard.

THE WHO & THE WHY

Place the stuffed dates on a table. Say: **This fun message time will be all about important firsts and about the New Testament man who accomplished these first time things. His name was John the Baptist, and he was a prophet who dressed in a camel-hair robe and ate locusts and wild honey. Before we discover more about John the Baptist, let's get in the mood by munching some tasty locusts and honey, as John the Baptist did!**

After kids' "ickys" and "oohs" subside, serve the pretend locusts and honey. Say: **Of course, these are pretend locusts and honey, but John probably did eat dates and honey during his life. John was born a few months before Jesus, and most people agree they were cousins. As John grew, God had an important plan for his life. John was to become the powerful voice that would prepare the people for Jesus.** Read aloud Matthew 3:1-6, then continue: **John brought us many firsts during his life. He became John the Baptist when he called people to the Jordan River to be baptized in the water to symbolize repentance and cleansing from sin.** Invite a volunteer to read the first item on the newsprint list, then use the blue marker write a number 1 beside it. Say: **In Old Testament times, priests would wash in running water to cleanse and purify themselves on the outside. But John the Baptist called for ordinary people to repent of their sins and be washed clean to show a willing and clean heart on the inside. John was the first to call for repentance in preparing our hearts for Jesus!**

John the Baptist was also the first to recognize Jesus as Lord and as God's Lamb. When Jesus began his ministry, he came to be baptized by John. John looked up and recognized Jesus coming toward him. Read aloud John 1:29. Have someone read the next item on the list and write a number 1 beside it. John the Baptist was the first person to call Jesus the "Son of God." Read aloud John 1:34, then have a volunteer write a number 1 beside item three on the list as it's read aloud. Continue: John the Baptist recognized that Jesus was sent by God to forgive our sins. He spent his entire life preaching about Jesus and his power to forgive our sins. But his life was cut short when he was beheaded by wicked King Herod, who hated John the Baptist for the things he said about Jesus and about his own wife, Queen Herodias. So John the Baptist became the first person to die in association with Jesus. Have a volunteer read item three on the list and place a number 1 beside it.

Say: **John the Baptist was God's prophet and the one God chose to warn others about making their paths straight through baptism and repentance of sins. John paved the way for Jesus in our hearts and lives. He may have dressed in odd clothing and have eaten some funky foods, but John the Baptist was "right on" when he told us to prepare for Jesus and his awesome love and forgiveness!** If there's time and enough goodies left, let kids stuff another round of "locusts and honey" to enjoy.

Distribute the Who's Who John the Baptist cards and invite a volunteer to read the card aloud. Punch holes in the corners of the cards and add them to the kids' Who's Who flip rings. If there's time, review any cards previously collected.

Who Was BARNABAS?

Acts 11:22-24; 1 Thessalonians 5:11

Simple Supplies: You'll need a Bible, scissors, a bag or small basket, copies of the Encouragement Cards from page 45, and copies of the Who's Who Barnabas card from page 46.
Before class, copy the Encouragement Cards from page 45 and cut the cards apart. Place the cards in a bag or basket. Finally, write the name "Barnabas" on the Who's Who board (directions on page 4) or on the chalkboard.

THE WHO & THE WHY

Gather kids and hold up the basket or bag containing the Encouragement Cards. Say: **I have cards here that have encouraging words on them. What is encouragement, and when is a time someone encouraged you?** Prompt kids to share their thoughts and experiences, then say: **It's very important to be a good encourager to others, for when we offer encouragement we offer help and understanding. In a moment, we'll act out these cards with partners to see what kinds of encouragement we can offer others. But first let's learn about a man in the New Testament whose name meant "son of encouragement."**

This man's name was Barnabas, and he came to accept Jesus soon after Jesus died and was risen again. Barnabas, like Paul, was a Jew who knew that Jesus was God's Son and had been sent to die for our sins. Barnabas wanted to use any gifts God had given him to serve Jesus. What was Barnabas's gift? His name told it all! Barnabas had the gift of encouragement, and God helped Barnabas use his special gift to bring others to Jesus and encourage them to grow in their faith.

Barnabas traveled on missionary trips with Paul and spent his time helping to establish churches. Barnabas lived up to his name by bringing powerful encouragement and hope to new Christians and saw many people baptized and become believers. Read aloud Acts 11:23. Say: **Barnabas was a good man, filled with the Holy Spirit and great faith.** Read aloud Acts 11:24, then continue: **It was Barnabas who helped establish the church at Antioch, where Jesus' followers were first called "Christians." Barnabas spent his life encouraging others in the Christian faith and bringing them to Jesus. Barnabas encouraged Paul as he labored to establish churches and bring others the Good News. And Barnabas is an encouragement to us today as a power-packed example of being God's servant.** Ask:

➤ *How did Barnabas's encouragement reflect his strong faith?*
➤ *In what ways can someone's encouragement help strengthen our faith when we're discouraged?*
➤ *What can we do to encourage others to have strong faith? to bring others to Jesus?*

Have kids get with partners to act out the Encouragement Cards for the class. Each card tells one way to encourage someone and is based on a Scripture verse. After each card is guessed (or after a minute or two of acting out the cards), read aloud each verse in the Bible.

Distribute the Who's Who Barnabas cards and invite a volunteer to read the card aloud. Punch holes in the corners of the cards and add them to the kids' Who's Who flip rings. If there's time, review any cards previously collected.

PAUL

PHARISEES

	Keeping Score													
Names	Make a slash mark for each blooper you make													

MARY

THANK YOU, MOM!

With all that you give me and all that you do,
You're a gift from heaven above,
For through you I know it must be true:
"Mother" is God's special word for LOVE!

BARNABAS

Pray for each other. (James 5:16)	**Be patient in troubles.** (Romans 12:11)
Serve one another in love. (Galatians 5:13)	**Honor one another above yourselves.** (Romans 12:10)
Be kind and compassionate to one another. (Ephesians 4:32)	**Please your neighbor to build him up.** (Romans 15:2)
Be devoted to one another. (Romans 12:10)	**Overcome evil with good.** (Romans 12:21)

WHO'S WHO CARDS

Angels

Angels are spiritual beings who act in the Bible as messengers of God's will and as his divine protectors. Angels announced Jesus' birth to shepherds and aided Peter's miraculous escape from prison. (Psalm 91:11, 12)

Apostles

Apostles learned about Jesus, then shared the Good News with others. Jesus first called twelve disciples, but later many apostles spread the gospel and started churches. (Matthew 4:19)

Barnabas

Barnabas, whose name means "son of encouragement," was a great encouragement to Paul. Barnabas helped establish the first church at Antioch, where Jesus' followers were first called "Christians." (Acts 11:23, 24)

Centurion

This Roman soldier didn't worship God or Jesus, but when he heard about Jesus' power, he asked Jesus to heal his servant. Jesus did, then said the centurion's faith was greater than anyone in Israel. (Matthew 8:5-13)

Gentiles

Gentiles were people who were not part of the Jewish nation. Through Jesus' love and forgiveness, God's grace was offered to both Jews and Gentiles—to anyone who accepts Jesus. (Romans 3:29)

Holy Spirit

Jesus promised the Holy Spirit as our helper, friend, Counselor, and guide. After Jesus was risen to heaven, he sent the Holy Spirit in a great rushing of wind to guide and empower us to accomplish God's will. (John 16:7-14)

John the Baptist

John the Baptist was Jesus' cousin and spent his life calling people to repent of their sins and to be baptized to make their hearts and lives ready for Jesus. (Matthew 3:1-6)

Joseph

Joseph was the husband of Mary and the earthly father of Jesus. Joseph was a carpenter from the city of Nazareth who loved and obeyed God and kept young Jesus safe from harm. (Matthew 1:24)

WHO'S WHO CARDS

Joseph of Arimathea

This Jewish religious leader from the city of Arimathea secretly became a follower of Jesus. After Jesus' death, Joseph cared for Jesus' body and provided his burial tomb. (John 19:38-42)

Lazarus

Lazarus was a beloved friend of Jesus and lived with his sisters, Mary and Martha. When Lazarus became ill and died, Jesus was so saddened that he raised Lazarus to life again. (John 11:26, 35, 41-44)

Lydia

Lydia sold expensive purple cloth in the city of Philippi. She was a Gentile who didn't know Jesus until she heard Paul tell the gospel. Lydia was baptized, then helped bring her family to know Jesus as well. (Acts 16:14, 15)

Martha

Martha lived with her sister Mary and her brother Lazarus. Martha taught us the importance of welcoming Jesus. She also learned from Jesus that it is important to be still and learn from him. (Luke 10:38-42)

Mary

Mary was the young woman God chose to give birth to his Son, Jesus. Mary encouraged Jesus to perform his first miracle at Cana and was Jesus' only family member present at his death on the cross. (Luke 1:46-49)

Paul

Saul spent his early life persecuting Jesus' followers. After Jesus' resurrection, he called to Saul on the road to Damascus. Saul's name was changed to Paul, and his life was changed to bring others to Jesus. (Acts 9:3-5)

Peter

Peter was the first disciple Jesus called. Though he denied he knew Jesus three times, Peter eventually became the one Jesus called "the rock" and on whom his church would be built. (Matthew 16:18)

Pharisees

The Pharisees were Jewish religious leaders who added their own "oral laws" to God's laws. The Pharisees spent much of their time judging others and did not get along with Jesus. (Matthew 5:17-20)

WHO'S WHO CARDS

Poor Widow

The widow at the temple was very poor and could only put two coins in the offering plate. Even though others put much more in, Jesus said the widow gave more because she gave all she had. (Mark 12:41-44)

Shepherds

Shepherds Jesus' day and were known for tending and protecting their flocks with their lives. Jesus referred to shepherds many times in his lessons and even called himself the Good Shepherd. (John 10:15)

Stephen

Stephen accepted Jesus sometime after Jesus' resurrection. He bravely told others about Jesus' plan for salvation and was later stoned to death for his loyalty to Jesus, becoming the first Christian martyr. (Acts 6:8; 7:51-53)

Thomas

Thomas, one of Jesus' twelve disciples, couldn't believe Jesus had been raised from death and wanted to see with his own eyes. Jesus appeared to Thomas and told him we are blessed when we believe without seeing. (John 20:29)

Wise Men

The wise men are traditionally understood to be three wise seers or kings who traveled from the East to worship baby Jesus and bring him special gifts of gold, frankincense, and myrrh. (Matthew 2:1-11)

Woman at the Well

This woman from Samaria was someone Jews would never talk with, but Jesus told her about his living water that lasts forever. He also forgave the woman of her sins. (John 4:7-14)

Zacchaeus

Zacchaeus was a tax collector who stole extra money from people. He was greatly disliked until Jesus accepted Zacchaeus and forgave him. Zacchaeus returned four times the money he had stolen. (Luke 19:1-10)